In a Dream You Saw a Way to Survive

ALSO BY CLEMENTINE VON RADICS

Mouthful of Forevers

For Teenage Girls with Wild Ambitions and Trembling Hearts

In a Dream You Saw a Way to Survive

CLEMENTINE VON RADICS

Andrews McMeel
PUBLISHING®

Contents

PART I

1

PART II

45

Index . . . 77

Acknowledgments . . . 81

About the author . . . 83

I've polished this anger and now it's a knife.
—Cathy Linh Che

In the dream, I cut open my own arm
and out poured a river that snaked its way
through Oregon. Out poured each dead friend,
now buried in the fall
earth which smells always of rot.

The blackberry stains,
the unswallowed medicine,
the face of each person I love
and hope to never see again.

Out poured each grief I have named
and each grief there is no language for.

In the dream, I saw a way to survive and I did.
This is how I remember it. I lost a whole river.
I stayed standing.

PART I

The first time I knew

I say to my best friend

*This love has become
an endless game
of cat and mouse.*

She says

Baby, I love you

But why are you always the mouse?

Storm.

The week
after I found
another woman's fingerprints
all over my home.

After the storm
of begging
and bended knees
had passed

a tornado hit the coast of Oregon.

The wind howling
like it had something to grieve.

Back home, a tree branch
crashed through my mother's window.
and isn't that how
it always goes?

You spend years building a home
just to watch it destroyed in seconds.

In the time it takes to say

*I'm sorry, I didn't want you to
find out
like this,
but she loves me.*

O,

Love.

Please convince me
of the storm that grew
between her mouth
and yours.

Convince me of its worth.
Please, one last lie,
I mean gift, I mean
reason enough, please,
convince me
to forgive you.

Now
you speak
and just like that
there is a paintbrush in your hand.

Just like that you paint this girl
into all of our memories.

You say *I love you*
and she is forming the words
and turning your neck.

You say *I'm sorry*
a howling thump unrelenting
against my front door
and she is kneeling beside you,
uncurling your fist.

There we are,
sleeping in our bed.

You reach for me
tuck your body into mine
and she stands in the corner.
A graceless smirk. Sweet,
thick, drenched in the truth.
and wasn't this always
my worst fear?

My love in glittering pieces all over the floor.
My trust just another mess that ruins the carpet.

Your girl,
a madness haunting my home.

She smiles
and a bitter shroud
falls across the bathroom mirror.
She says your name
and cockroaches crawl
inside the walls.

I tell you to leave
and it is so cold here now.

The wind
keeps howling against my window

over and over and
over.

As if to tell me
one more thing
I don't want to hear.

You apologize for your mistake.

But the mistake was mine
for trusting you.

You apologize
like I haven't met a stranger
on the train, followed them home,
let them ruin my skin on the carpet.

The question was in my mouth too,
love,
I just kept it there.

For the last five nights I've had dreams about the woman he left me for.

In these dreams,
I am always scrambling to take care of her
somehow. Offering her a warm meal,
a soft blanket, a sturdy pair of shoes
but of course, awake, I have done nothing
or worse.

When he said
>*I made a mistake,*
>*let me try*
>*and come*
>
>*back to you*

I said
>*Yes.*

I said
>*Come.*

I said
>*Leave her bed*
>*cold. Come home to me*
>*I will become the kind of woman*
>*who can forgive you.*

I said that.

As if it could ever be that simple.

There is a better version of this story
where we both leave him.

Instead of loving him so much it felt like church.
Building a cathedral inside his crooked mouth.
Tossing our crooked prayers inside.

We are so alike, she and I.

What do we know
but devotion?

She hates me now.

And I respect her for it.

At least one of us has the sense
to stay the hero in her own story.
To name someone the wolf
in the parable.

To take his teeth from him,
leave their bloody business
to my mouth. I asked for this
after all, then asked for it
again.

Theories on Why I'm Like This

BECAUSE I'VE GOT THIN SKIN AND BAD LUCK.

BECAUSE GHOSTS DIZZY THEMSELVES ABOVE ME,
LIKE ME BEST, AND TOUCH ME FIRST.
THEIR VOICES AN OLD SONG I KEEP
RATTLING AROUND IN MY BRAIN.

BECAUSE EVERY TIME SOMEONE OFFERS ME
THEIR BODY, I CONVINCE MYSELF TO CALL IT HOME.

BECAUSE ENOUGH PEOPLE HURT ME
AND I CONVINCED MYSELF
I AM A PERSON WHO DESERVED TO BE HURT.

BECAUSE EVERY TIME YOU BROKE A WINDOW
I SWEPT THE GLASS.

I SAY YOUR NAME,
AND THE AUDIENCE SHIFTS IN THEIR SEATS.

I say your name,
and I've raised the dead.

O you, reckless anarchist.
Arsonist of our lives.

I say your name and become
the dead.

This grief opens my mouth
and speaks your name.

Listen,

to say it wasn't all bad is the truth
and a disservice to the truth.
You, untamed flame.
My whole face is a white flag.
I'll hold it up for you.
Only you.

The Fear

All my friends are tired
of knowing what it is
I'm going to say
before I say it.

I am afraid
I will love you forever
and we will never be
in the same room
again.

I swear, next time I see you I'll be funny.

I will make jokes at my own expense,
be charming as a surprise.
I will ask about your new life
and Be Cool About It
and I will not mention Memphis.
Or how your hair feels in my hands.
I will not mention the last time I saw you.
My mouth, so far from yours, I said
I am afraid I will spend entire years
trying not to need you.
As if I wasn't certain.
As if this wasn't my confession.

Ever the optimist.

He tells me he does not
want to think about the past,
only the future.

                                        What a short life the bullet has
                                              compared to the wound.

What I would give
to leave the past behind
and have it stay there.

Confession:

By the time
you gave me
a diamond necklace,

I loved it more
than my own throat.

Somewhere in Oregon a scattering of men are smiling despite what they have done.

I pull their names out of my skin
Like strange, poison strings.

I lay them on my sheets and the bed opens
like the mouth of the strange beast.

Each bottle in my house starts to rattle.
Everything I have ever buried

eventually started to dance.

Post-term.

That winter I stopped being your wife
and became a pregnant hollow.
A swelling brood of
               Absence.

Why ask so much of an empty heart,
love?

        All the longing I do is for a dead thing.
        I open my mouth
        her hands fall out.

To the Protester Outside of the Clinic who Called Me a Murderer:

If I could have kept her, if she'd have been born a girl, I would have called her Jane. As in Austen. As in my sister's middle name and my grandmother's before her. I would have taught her to be kind. To be good. To love the Beach Boys even and especially after Brian got weird. I know you don't want to hear this. Prefer to think me faceless and bloodstained, another statistic on cruel, thoughtless women. But like everyone else, this was never going to be my choice until it had to be. When I fought for the right to choose, I thought I was fighting for other people. Thought this right necessary but rough-edged. And ugly. And never for me. But that was before the missed blood. Before the days spent bent and gagging. Before the doctor said *You're about four weeks along*. And why wasn't I more careful? Didn't I know what the medication I take can do to a baby? And that is how you and I met. Me walking into that clinic to do the hardest thing I've ever had to do. You. Finding a hundred ways to call me a killer for it.

Do you even remember my face?

Because I can't forget yours. I think of you. Constantly. Want to snatch the scream out of your mouth. Want to wrap my hand around your hand. Lower the sign that called me a killer. Tell you that my body was not a safe place for anyone. And even if it was, I wasn't ready to love a person the way they deserve to be loved once you build them out of nothing but your body and promise to protect them forever. If I could have spoken to you that day I would have told you that the thing I want most in this life is to be a mother. But I know now that's not true.

The thing I want most in this life is to be a good mother.

And I wasn't ready. So I said goodbye. I thought that was the kind of thing a good mother would do.

You are flying home today.

Back to Portland,
bringing your tongue
and all of the ways it has left me shaking.
Part of me does not want to pick you up
from the airport. I want to picture you
waiting at the arrivals gate for hours,
watching an endless flight of passengers
running toward tearful lovers.
A flock of outstretched arms
and none of them for you. You,
standing there with a whole life's
worth of heavy shit and no one
to help you carry it.

This is a selfish hope,
but what else do I have left to give
You, coming home, bringing your faith
in endless chances. You know
all about my stupid heart
and the place you hold inside it.
I put it in all the poems,
then put those poems down on paper,
read them aloud to strangers,
put them in books,
sent those books around the world.
I made news of my love,
like I was flyering for a lost dog.
Which, perhaps, I was.

A CONVERSATION BETWEEN MY THERAPIST AND THE MOUTH THAT SOMETIMES BELONGS TO ME:

Would you describe the mania
as watching a bird die on your doorstep
or the sensation of having wings?

> I want you to know the
> second time I went crazy
> there was no one to blame
> except my own soft burning
> brain.

Why does calling yourself sick
make you feel stronger?

> It doesn't. I just believe my
> crooked truth and I don't
> want it stolen from me. I
> have tasted colors you don't
> even know about but I
> understand why it's best
> to take such heroics away.
>
> I understand why
> people are better left unholy
> and on the ground.

IN A DREAM YOU SAW A WAY TO SURVIVE

On a scale of a snowstorm
to all the secrets of your womanhood
laid cracked, exposed
on the forest floor,
boiled into a soup, used to nourish,
how real would you say your hands are?

                     I don't sleep but when I do
                     I dream of the Oregon Trail,
                     thousands of strangers
                     crossing mountains to steal
                     the ground that became
                     my home.

                     Some of them passed with no
                     trouble but I don't think
                     about them.

When you divorce
the idea of your body from your body
what color is the escape velocity
hurtling you toward
the stomach of the universe?

                     Don't you think about
                     the Donner Party?

>Doesn't it bother you that
>children ate soup made
>from the legs of their dead
>father for the privilege
>of this land?
>
>What do you call the children
>of such a story?

Let's try and stay
in this room. Now,
if I were to crack your skull
open how many Gods and
Daughters and cockroaches
would spring fully formed
from your soft burning
brain?

>Why am I always asked
>to describe my madness
>as though this condition was
>not the absence of reason
>and its language?

What would you say to him
if he were here right now?

> I want you to know
> when I buried the hatchet
> I gave it a proper funeral
> and everything.

I think we call this progress.

> But what do you call the
> children? Is this the way a
> wolf becomes a dog? Listen.
> There was once a terrible
> snow and I ate despite,
> I made soup from my own
> bones.

His new girlfriend thinks I'm crazy.

And I guess,
for her sake

I hope that she's right.

I hope the world unspools itself.
restrings a new truth. Camel
through the eye of a needle.

I hope for her
and her good heart
that I and every girl
who tried to warn me
are just jealous.

I hope the truth
untruths itself

and we all become liars.
strung out Him-junkies
angry to have lost our fix.

Do it, girl.
call us all liars
while you call yourself lucky.

Lord knows
I sang that song for years.

Lord knows

it's easier to love a smiling man
than the woman between his teeth.

Echo.

There is a song by a band I can't remember,
but I know The Donnas covered it.

> *When I said that I loved you,*
> *I meant that I'd love you forever.*

When I said that I loved you
I'm not sure what I meant
but know I meant it in the spirit
of all great love songs:

inexact, but with great feeling.

Let me tell you about the future:

There is no monument
to your breaking jaw
or all my different names
for mending. and look,
across a handful of rivers:
you, on one knee.

Her beautiful body
growing children
who do not have my eyes.

Do you understand?

All of this coming together and
apart, our ever-gasping communion
it's just the echo of an old song.

Or if it is not
I'm still certain I cannot love you

and forgive us your sins
at the same time.

I say all this but listen
the record scratches
the same moment

asking the air
for itself again.

Bitter.

I hated him most
for not having the courage
to ruin us grandly.
To break all the dishes
and burn down the house.
Instead he sunk quiet
into new arms, called
her my name, each
devotion repurposed.

Denied me my spilled blood,
my great war.
except his confession.

Still we swing.

It is the summer of 2006 and we are in a Buick the color of an old bruise. Mackayla's boyfriend just said *Only bitches go to river beaches* and he doesn't mean bitches the way I mean it but I am not about to say shit about that while perched on the edge of the window, arms and torso reckless with wind, my legs above the backseat, gripped tightly in Jordyn's arms, as this boy swings down back roads going eighty and we called this Freedom instead of Stupid or Something, Anything To Do.

We pass the place where happy people swim, park crooked in the dirt beneath where the overpass holds the river.

In this corner of the valley, ropes dangle from every tree like birthday streamers. There is only an inch between water deep enough to dive in and your prom photo ending up on the news

and still we swing

from each fraying neon cord into the cold yelp of August. What we must have looked like then. Our dirty scramble of discount limbs. A spread of needles left in the dust. A scream where a family should be.

Years later, after Mackayla's baby but before her DUI, I read an article about the forest service removing all the ropes from the river's edge. Half of them already cut

too short to swing from by the hand of someone who
watched their friend or child meet the brutal end of a rock.
Swallowed by our river.

Which is, coincidentally, exactly how I learned to say *I
love you* back home. To give as much warning as you can
without words, just a blade and a steady hand. How often
we left it all up to a warning we did not give

and look
how much good it did us.

A bird flew

I.

When my uncle died,
we held a funeral for him
and four people came.
He spent the last decade of his life
Drunk, living in a van
in the Fred Meyer parking lot,
but before that
he lived with my family.
When I was little
he taught me how to read,
how to make pancakes,
that the birds
in our neighborhood
were doves,
and how to kill them
with a well-thrown rock.
But with each passing year
he became more dead dove
more flightless thing
more ghost
haunting living body.
After he got knocked
out of every bar in town
he couldn't stay
at our house anymore,
he washed up at our door
one too many times
slushmouthed and bloody.

II.

This man is my family.
He bought me a new book
every year on my birthday

even in the cold years
he could barely buy food.

It's shocking, isn't it?

The people we love
and all the different people
they can be.

He died two years ago.
I said his name this morning.

I swear,
somewhere a dove flew
before it met with a rock.

Listen closely

it is the last
you will ever hear from me

Even in my dreams
I do not follow you

I belong more to my own survival
than to you
and the fiction of permanence.

Eventually

Each exaltation
flew backwards
into my mouth
and swallowed itself.

Notes on the term survivor:

I need you to know
I loved him enough
to lie to everyone who knew me
about how bad it got.

I need you to know
there is still a bullet
lodged between my ribs
in the shape of his holy mouth.

I need you to know
the night the neighbors saw
what they did, when I took
back my voice

finally found the strength
to call him a monster,
I woke up the next morning
and I did not feel brave.

I woke up feeling
like the love of my life

        is a monster

which is the opposite of triumph.

Which is the whole world
Dropped. Clattering
across the hardwood floor.

We talk about survival
like it's a thing that makes you
stronger.

Like it is a lesson learned.
As if it does not steal your truth
fashion it into a killing machine.

As if a thing that does not kill you
makes you more than a person
who is not killed.

But I remember
I remember everything.
I was a bird before this.

Now,
a graveyard
of the unburied.

My healing is ugly.
My edges cracked and uninspiring.

But still, they are my edges.
Still, I am healing.

Isn't that itself a song?
A chorus of rage and gentle

worthy of a dance.

Say Survivor.

Say it with it's whole
unbearable weight.

and say it again.

and say amen.

Say amen.

I NO LONGER BELIEVE ANGER
WILL SAVE ME.

For that,
I have to put down the knife.
I have to thank my breath.
I have to let you go.

In the dream, what became too heavy
to carry—the blackberry stains,
the unswallowed medicine,
the face of each person, each bruise healed
so many colors it had become a sunset
and this is the story of the way the ocean
fell in love with the moon.

In the dream, I saw a way to survive and I was full
of Joy. If it is true, that all we leave behind are the
stories we tell, then this is how I remember it.
From me there flowed a whole river,
and the ground itself took a breath.

PART II

You are on the floor crying.

And you have been
on the floor crying
for days.

And that is you
being brave.
That is you getting through it
as best you know how.

No one else can decide
What your tough looks like.

Carrie a nation.

During Prohibition,
the activist Carrie Nation
legally changed her name
to Carrie A. Nation. As in,
she believed she was going to

> *Carry a nation away*
> *from the plague of*
> *alcoholism*

She believed she was

> *a bulldog*
> *running along*
> *at the heels*
> *of Jesus, barking*
> *at whatever*
> *He doesn't like*

Her whole deal was
getting men
who loved whiskey
to just, like, stop.

Historians believe
that many of the women
who fought for prohibition

did so because of what
alcohol had done
to their men.

You can't declare war on grief. You can't
declare war on loss, or

what a husband's hands do
when the door is closed,

but you can declare war
on liquor. You can take it from
his drying mouth, pray it's the cause
and not the symptom.

                        The first man Carrie
                        A. Nation ever loved drank
                        himself to death
                        a week before
                        their daughter was born.

For the next fifty years,
she walked into bars
all across Kansas
armed with an ax
and just started
breaking shit.

I'm not saying that's ok.

                I'm just saying
                I've seen a mirror before.

I'm saying I loved a man for years
thinking he was the bandage
only to realize he was the wound.

                I'm saying I get it.

Grief is a beast
with many faces.
Sometimes it looks like
the first cry of
a fatherless child.

                Sometimes, like
                reaching for an ax.

Angie.

I will not write another poem
about your body. How we found it.
How it is not your body anymore
and has disappeared
into new purpose.
There is sorrow, yes.
Sometimes I can't breathe for it.
Sometimes it folds up easy;
waits until I am ready
to consider its weight.
I am often ready these days.
In death, you have become
the simplest version of yourself.
I catch myself sorting memories,
piecing together your life in a way
that adds up to your end.
In truth, I did not know you well.
But we bruised in the same places.
I saw myself in your stories and knew
we were not alone. I loved you once.
Now, when the world narrows
to the most simple beauties:
When I am dancing in Berlin,
or hiking the Grand Canyon,
or listening to a song we both once loved,
I speak your name out loud.
And in that way you are still here.
Taking in the world for all the good
it has left to offer you,

clasping the day with shaking fingers.
For a moment, you are with me,
with all of us, back with the world
you left. Our lives still tumbling forward,
drenched in you, chanting your name.

Split.

After buying me a third beer
this man, who has been my ex
five years longer than he was my lover
asks me if I'm

*like, all the way gay now
since I have, you know,
a girlfriend
or whatever.*

I wink.

I laugh the kind of laugh
That always breaks him in half.

*She's not my girlfriend or whatever
anymore.* I say. Touching his knee.
An orchestrated accident. He smiles,
his mouth a bowl of spilled cream.
Of course it's true. I'm not like,
all the way gay. I love men.
Who doesn't love a game
they know exactly how to win.

I bet she is somewhere
slicing tomatoes framed by sunlight.
Of course I dream of owning the mouth
that splits her open. Still, I've lived
inside my own heart for a long time now.

I know what I do when I am lonely
and need proof of my body.

This crooked night ends in a bright morning.
Interrupted by a dream where I become
the light that warms her. A bird
with a scorched throat.

Mantra.

You are a church
of broken glass
and hallelujahs.

You are haunted
like every other holy thing.

What tried to destroy you
didn't have the strength.

Still you stand.
Sturdy and smelling of smoke.

On punching the dude who tried to pull me out of the pit:

I imagine this is what it is like to be a man.
Or at least some men.
Or a bird.
Anything free, really.
Unconcerned with its own face.
To be a woman
is to be so burdened by the body
you bury yourself
inside it.

Still, I dream
of taking up space.
Of being as solid
as the boy with his grip
on my wrist.
My grandfather, he built
my mother
a table in 1983.
She carved
all her favorite bands
into it,
I keep it in my kitchen
now. A mosaic
of everything
that once howled manic
through the Castro.

In this pit
I throw my bones
into the ocean of bodies

and the ocean
spits back

> *This music is the first*
> *is the only good gift*
> *of your blood.*
>
> *His howl in your throat*
> *owns you more*
> *than your own name.*

Punk is nothing
if not a bareknuckle fight
against anything Stronger
and Bigger
and Stealing from you

so I throw my fist
into the fucker trying to rob me
of my only home.

*This is for
my Mother's heart,*

I say,

Lost as it may be.

I'm gonna bite the bullet.

I mean, the apple. I mean,

I know
what you want to do
to me

and I am not afraid of snakes.

For Vincent van Gogh, Patron Saint of Psychotic Manic Depressives.

Often, I think of Vincent
and the meat that was once his ear.
How he gave it to a pretty girl
who was not certain of his name
and then spent the night alone
trying not to bleed to death.

Ever since my own diagnosis

some part of me
is always alive
and inside that moment.

I picture that scared girl,
the bleeding painter
the jagged flesh
between them.

Sometimes I am the girl.
Sometimes I am the dripping blood.
But most often
I am the one
offering up
some unwanted mess
of my self
and calling it a gift.

On the worst days
to be manic depressive

is to stand on ground
that can't promise to stay
beneath you.

It is to be both violence
and victim,

both the knife
and flesh
that welcomes it in.

So often
in these poems
in a lover's bed
at my mother's kitchen table
I offer up the truth of this
and watch the people I love
pull themselves away
from me.

I am chaos.
A barely hidden bar fight.
I know exactly
how many people believe
I am impossible to love.

There are days I believe it too.
I am in love with a good person
they sleep beside me every night
and every time they say
they love me

My first thought is

> *why*
> *Can't you see all the nicer people*
> *with fewer problems?*

My second thought is

> *good*
> *Who else is going to love me*
> *if you decide to stop?*

It is so easy to lose myself
in the mess of this.
To say *I love you*
and mean only *I'm sorry.*

But I try to think about
Vincent van Gogh.

His first teacher said
only a madman could paint like that.
Only in madness could you hold
so much joy and grief
in the same paintbrush.

and in this thought
every drop of paint and blood
joins in the same river

like how every sunflower
burst like a star
from Vincent's wild heart.

They say his illness
is the reason
he saw the starry night sky
swirl like that

His illness became genius
which became
a revelation.

and thank the stars for that miracle.

For the way we work
our broken fingers
through the dirt
'til we convince the good
to grow there.

I have spent countless days
grieving my own brain
But tonight, I sing for its brilliance
in the way that only I can.

And praise the stars for that.

For this new joy.
For this good blood.

For the beauty I find
and the river it takes
to carry me there.

I will not apologize
for what allows me to see the sky.

Not tonight
Not ever again.

THEORIES OF MYTHIC CONSEQUENCE

I DIDN'T KNOW HOW TO TOUCH YOU,
SO I CAST NEW HANDS IN THE MUD
AND BURIED THEM IN YOUR HAIR.

YOU KISSED ME, AND THE EARTH
SHIFTED AN INCH. I LANDED IN THE
RIVER. TELL ME THE STORY OF WATER
WHICH IS AGAIN SO NEW.

> *THE RIVER LOST HER MOUTH*
> *IN A FLOOD. SHE THREADED*
> *HER FINGERS THROUGH THE MOUNTAINS*
> *AND LEARNED OF MANY WAYS TO SPEAK.*

WE FELL IN LOVE
AND LEFT THE WHOLE WORLD BEHIND.

I DON'T MISS IT.
IT WAS A BAD WORLD. NOW,
EVERY GROCERY LIST IS AN ODE
EACH TIME MY NEIGHBOR HUMS
MOON RIVER IT IS PROOF OF FLOWERS.

YOU HAVE ALTERED THE COURSE OF
THE UNIVERSE
BY ENTERING THE ROOM.

The Poet refuses to see what can be plainly seen.

This morning I woke up so in love with you I didn't know what to do with my body, which was far from yours. Your body being asleep in a different city in a bed I've never seen. At work, I locked the bathroom door and allowed myself five minutes to meditate on your skin beneath my tongue, I don't know how this happened. I just woke up one morning and you were the blood in all my poems.

Plato made up a story about love once. Trying as we all do to assign meaning to the longing of blood and muscle. He said that Before the world was the world each person was two people connected as one, sharing the churning bile of organs, which is to say whole.

In this ancient and blooming place, longing did not exist until Zeus grew jealous, splitting each person in half with a blade of lightning, and that was the birth of loneliness and fucking and longing and birth.

This is how we learned to search for each other, to clatter our bodies back into a single thing.

I like to imagine us like this, an androgynous animal feared by God itself. It explains why I miss you like a limb. It explains this hopeless longing I've got working through my blood.

At work, I close my eyes, imagine each way we could push ourselves together in defiance of lightning, demanding the impossible.

I Began to Believe in Magic

& During the months we were first falling in love
the world became oracular
& Denver became a palm, each street a line that
predicted our fate.
& At least once a week,
& only when we were together, we would come
across a cluster of ambulances.
& once, a crushed car. The other a fire.
& it is a thing we want to find meaning in so badly

> I decide the want is reason enough
> for its meaning. We find the sight of the
> catastrophe but only its aftermath. We find
> the tear as the universe pulls out the needle
> and thread.

This one is just a love poem.

The way he walks
is my favorite walk

The way he moves his hands
is my favorite way
that anyone,
in the history of the world
has ever moved their hands.

It was a thing I knew for certain

That night on the phone when you said *We Should Get Married* and I said *Yes* with such feeling that I fell out of a hammock, into the mud, and knew again the first time every part of my body was open to your mouth and you only stopped smiling to kiss my nose. It's what I'm trying for, when we are uncooked, half asleep, whispering that I feel silly, feel dizzy, feel I Never Want To Stop Touching You especially where you are most fragile.

Love, I am working toward the theory that a single truth is enough to right a life, like a candle in a dark room. I was wrong before when I said mean things about love songs. I'm sorry, love songs. For years I had memorized facts about stones and I did not want to be a thing that wants. But I wake up grateful to any misplaced God that brought me to you. I know now what the staggering beast in my chest is capable of when it meets an equally strange and gentle beast. Everything I wished for is true, and I was right to wish.

A Second Prayer

I hope
We raise children
who only yell
from joy.

Building an Altar
After Jessica Helen Lopez

I light a candle for Misha's first lipstick. Beside it,
our first kiss, her bare hands and beard
and breath, her body still in its boy costume.

I light a candle for each night
we fell asleep holding hands
wishing to wake up in each other's skin.

Each Yahrzeit, we have gathered lavender
and the pills of our dead friend.
These too, I offer.

Please, take my sister's hands, my mother's silence
the kitchen knives and honey and not the body
of womanhood, but the burden of it.

This is what I know of love. To forgive
each other our desires. You can build God
out of anything, if it's the only thing before you.

Denver

*"There are years that ask
and years that answer"*
—Zora Neale Hurston

and there are years
that talk all over each other
and have 1,000 tongues
and have expensive tongues
and there are years
that take 1,000 years
and years that take
the shape of hands
and there are years
that just take when you
get really unlucky
but, hopefully,
those years are few
and hurried out the door
by years like this
when we are so broke
but our window faces
a church garden so
gracious with kale
and sunflowers, where
I thought you were the answer
until I knew you were
the question, the whole

IN A DREAM YOU SAW A WAY TO SURVIVE

and truest question,
one I opened
like a garden
to greet.

The Last Poem

It's Tuesday, and my knees hurt
because they always hurt and tonight,
memory trips me up and dares me
to say something. Memory sits
like a dead dog in the corner.

Still, we pay the gas bill. I feed the cat.
I fix my lipstick, we put on our boots,
and head to the bar with the good happy hour
and the bartender with six fingers on his right hand
who always remembers our names.

Memory keeps knocking like a bad landlord.
I'm still here. I know this because it hurts
and I'm so grateful. I didn't plan to be alive
this long. I didn't plan to eat good food I bought
with poems. I didn't plan to bitch
about a kind of life I once believed impossible,
to trudge through the rain back to my home
with its full kitchen its full bookshelves,
sharing my bed with the kind of love
I used to close my eyes and wish for.

This life is such a heaven I forget to notice.
If I could tell my younger self anything
about this life: we do so much more
than just survive it.

Index

A bird flew *34*

About the author *81*

Acknowledgments *79*

A conversation between my therapist and the mouth that sometimes belongs to me: *23*

Angie. *51*

A Second Prayer *71*

Bitter. *31*

Building an Altar (*After Jessica Helen Lopez*) *72*

Carrie a nation. *48*

Confession: *17*

Denver *73*

Echo. *29*

Eventually *37*

Ever the optimist. *16*

For the last five nights I've had dreams about the woman he left me for. *9*

INDEX

For Vincent van Gogh, Patron Saint of
Psychotic Manic Depressives. *60*

His new girlfriend thinks I'm crazy. *27*

I Began to Believe in Magic *68*

I'm gonna bite the bullet. *59*

I no longer believe anger will save me. *41*

I say your name, and the audience shifts in their seats. *12*

I swear, next time I see you I'll be funny. *15*

It was a thing I knew for certain *70*

Listen, *13*

Listen closely *36*

Mantra. *55*

Notes on the term survivor: *38*

On punching the dude who tried to
pull me out of the pit: *56*

Post-term. *19*

Somewhere in Oregon a scattering of men are
smiling despite what they have done. *18*

Split. *53*

INDEX

Still we swing. *32*

Storm. *4*

The Fear *14*

The first time I knew *3*

The Last Poem *75*

The Poet refuses to see what can be plainly seen. *66*

This one is just a love poem. *69*

To the protester outside of the clinic who called me a murderer: *20*

You apologize for your mistake. *8*

You are flying home today. *22*

You are on the floor crying. *47*

Acknowledgments

Multiple poems in this book, as well as its title, were inspired by Jenny Holzer's truism: In A Dream You Saw A Way To Survive And You Were Full of Joy.

The poem *Altar* was written after a workshop with Jessica Helen Lopez.

Thank you, Patty Rice and the entire team at Andrews McMeel, for believing in me twice. Thank you, Shay Alexi, for your tender bitch brilliance. Thank you, Elizabeth von Radics, for being both my mom and my most eager copyeditor.

Thank you to the poets and people who helped bring this book into the world: Desiree Dallagiacomo, Jordan Cooley, Grace Akon, Samantha Slupski, Madison Mae Parker, Alex Montinola, Schuyler Bailar, Red Maenza, Lip, Allison Truj, Jane Belinda, Julia Gaskill, Doc Luben, Brenna Twohy, Devin Devine, and Sabrina Benaim.

Thank you, Misha. Thank you, Leja. For the edits and the guidance and everything else.

About the Author

Clementine von Radics is a writer and performer from Oregon. They are the author of several other collections including *Mouthful of Forevers* and *Dream Girl*. Clementine lives in Brooklyn, New York.

In a Dream You Saw a Way to Survive copyright © 2019 by Clementine von Radics. All rights reserved. Printed in the United States of America. No part of this book may be used or reproduced in any manner whatsoever without written permission except in the case of reprints in the context of reviews.

Andrews McMeel Publishing
a division of Andrews McMeel Universal
1130 Walnut Street, Kansas City, Missouri 64106

www.andrewsmcmeel.com

19 20 21 22 23 BVG 10 9 8 7 6 5 4 3 2 1

ISBN: 978-1-5248-5061-6

Library of Congress Control Number: 2019930755

Editor: Patty Rice
Designer/Art Director: Diane Marsh
Production Editor: Margaret Daniels
Production Manager: Carol Coe

Illustrations by Shay Alexi

Attention: Schools and Businesses
Andrews McMeel books are available at quantity discounts with bulk purchase for educational, business, or sales promotional use. For information, please e-mail the Andrews McMeel Publishing Special Sales Department: specialsales@amuniversal.com.